Sheer & Lace

Hot Sexy Lingerie Girls
Models Pictures

By **PHOTO ART LOVER**

Copyright © Sheer & Lace

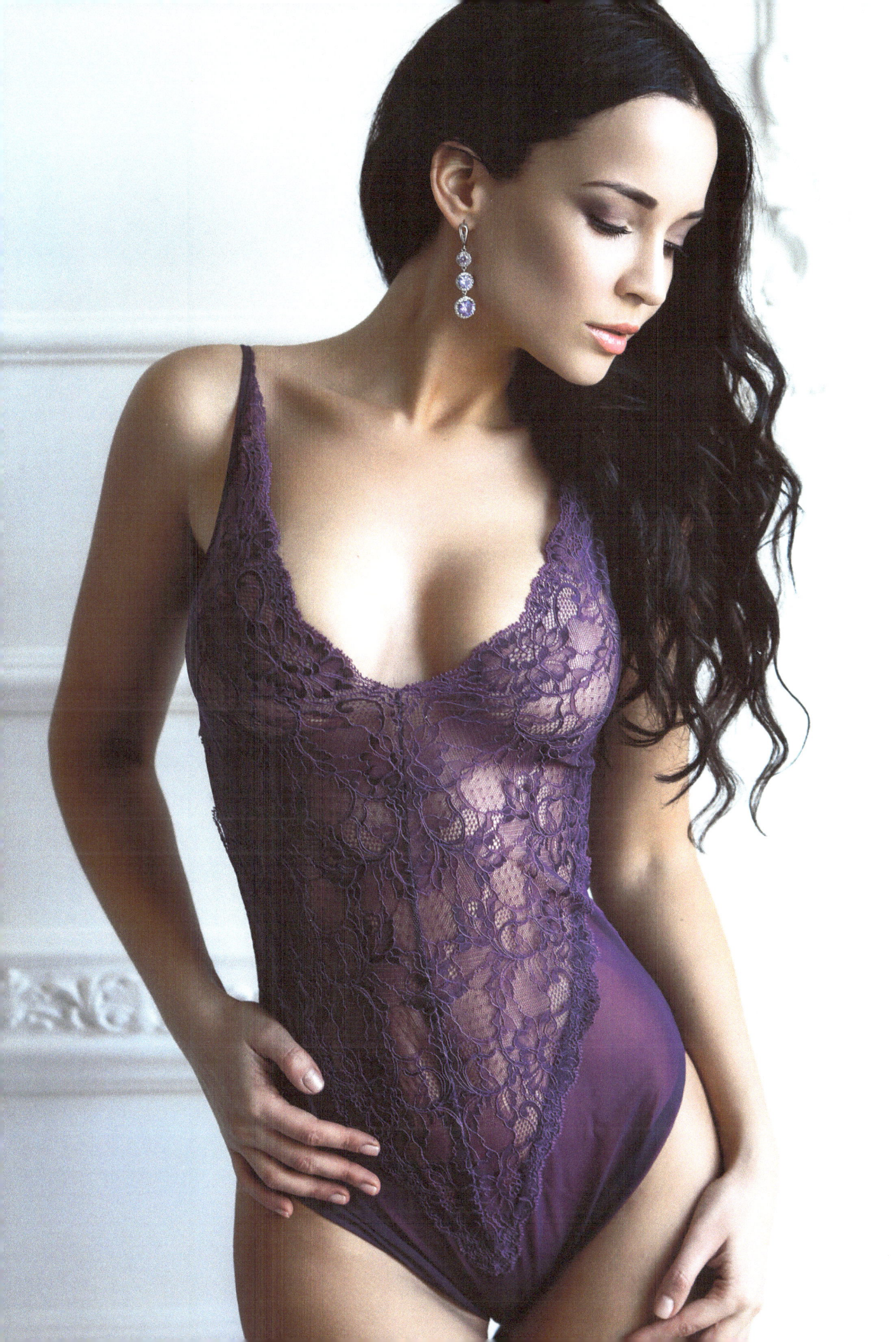

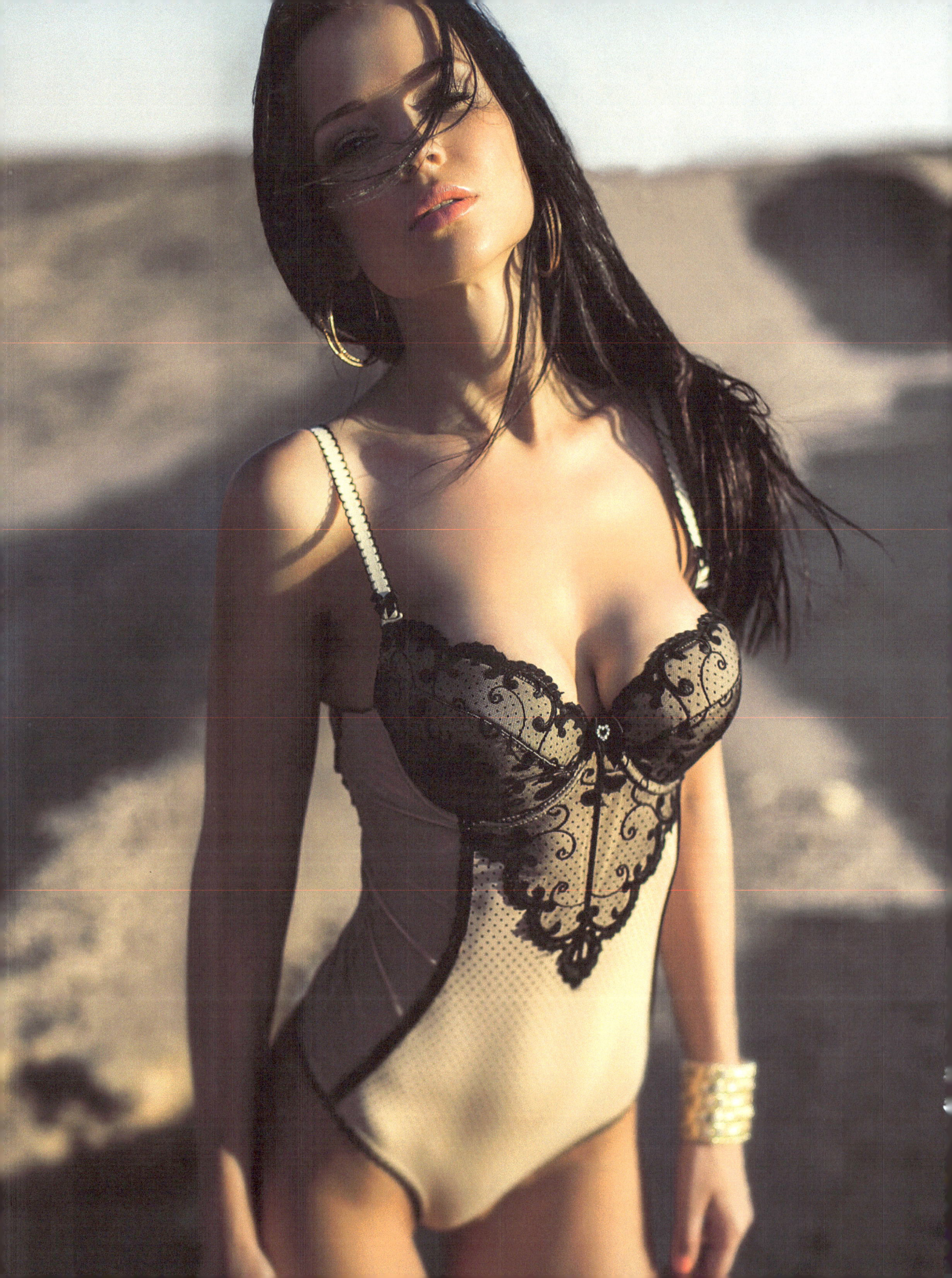

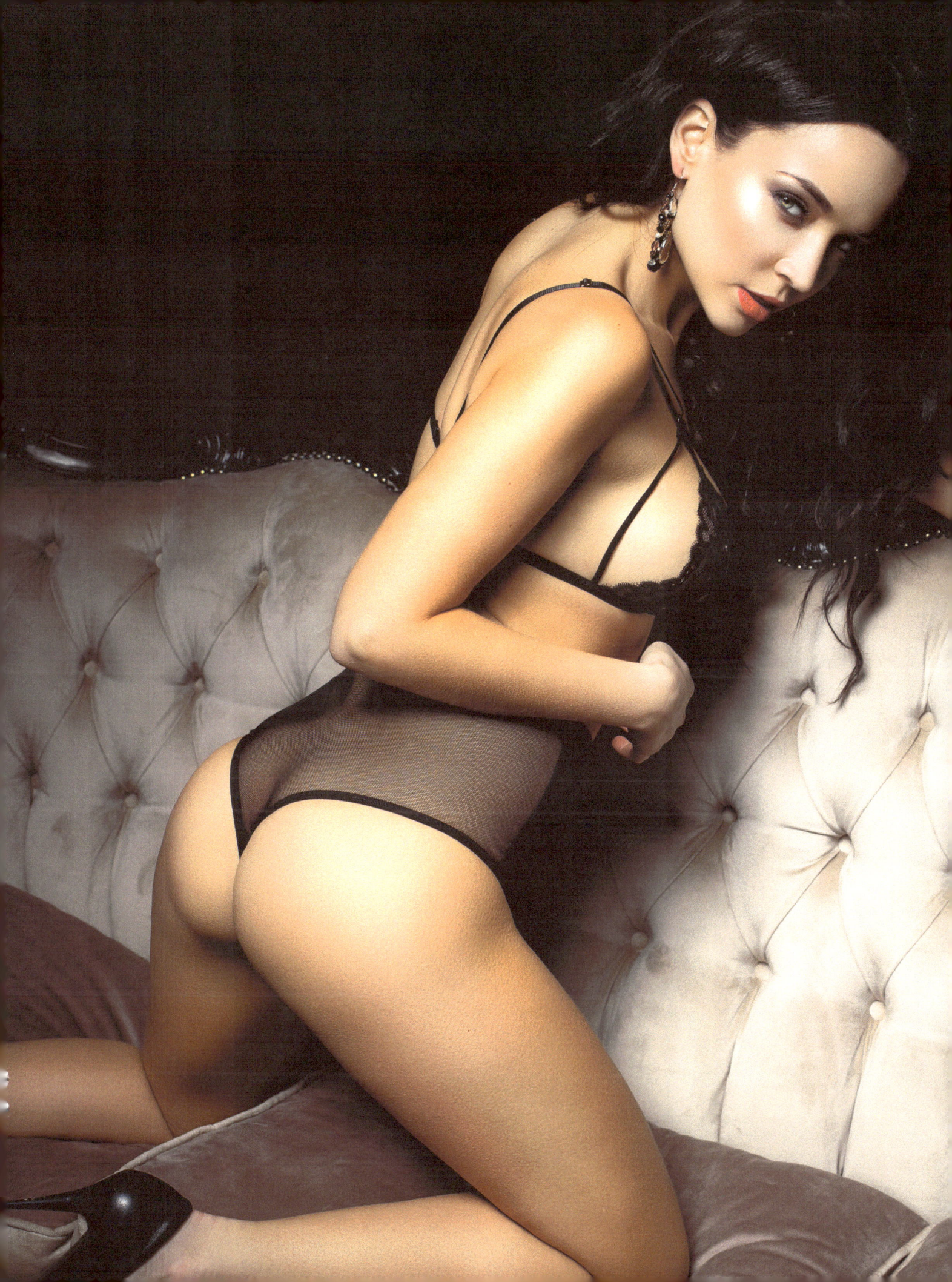

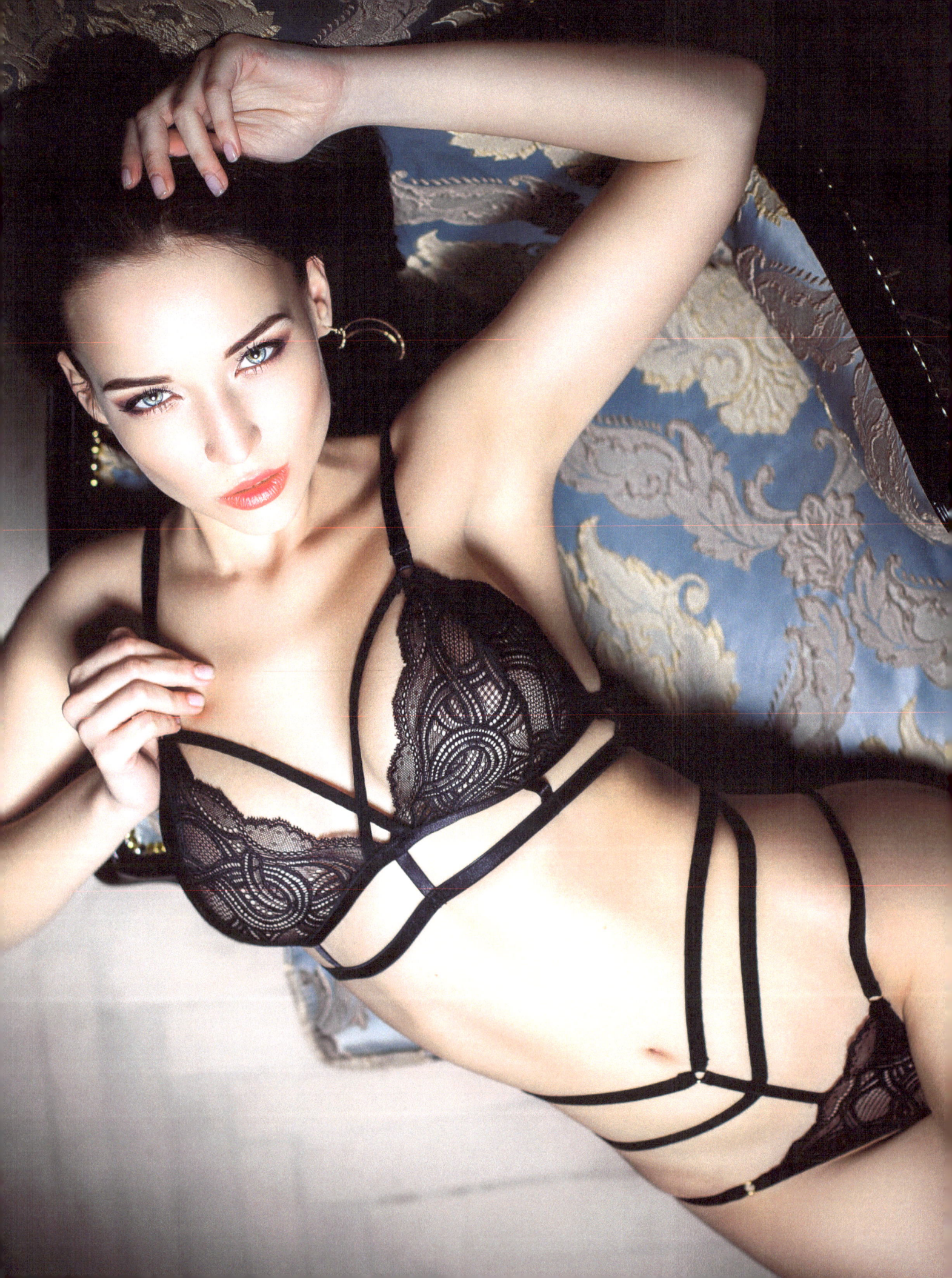

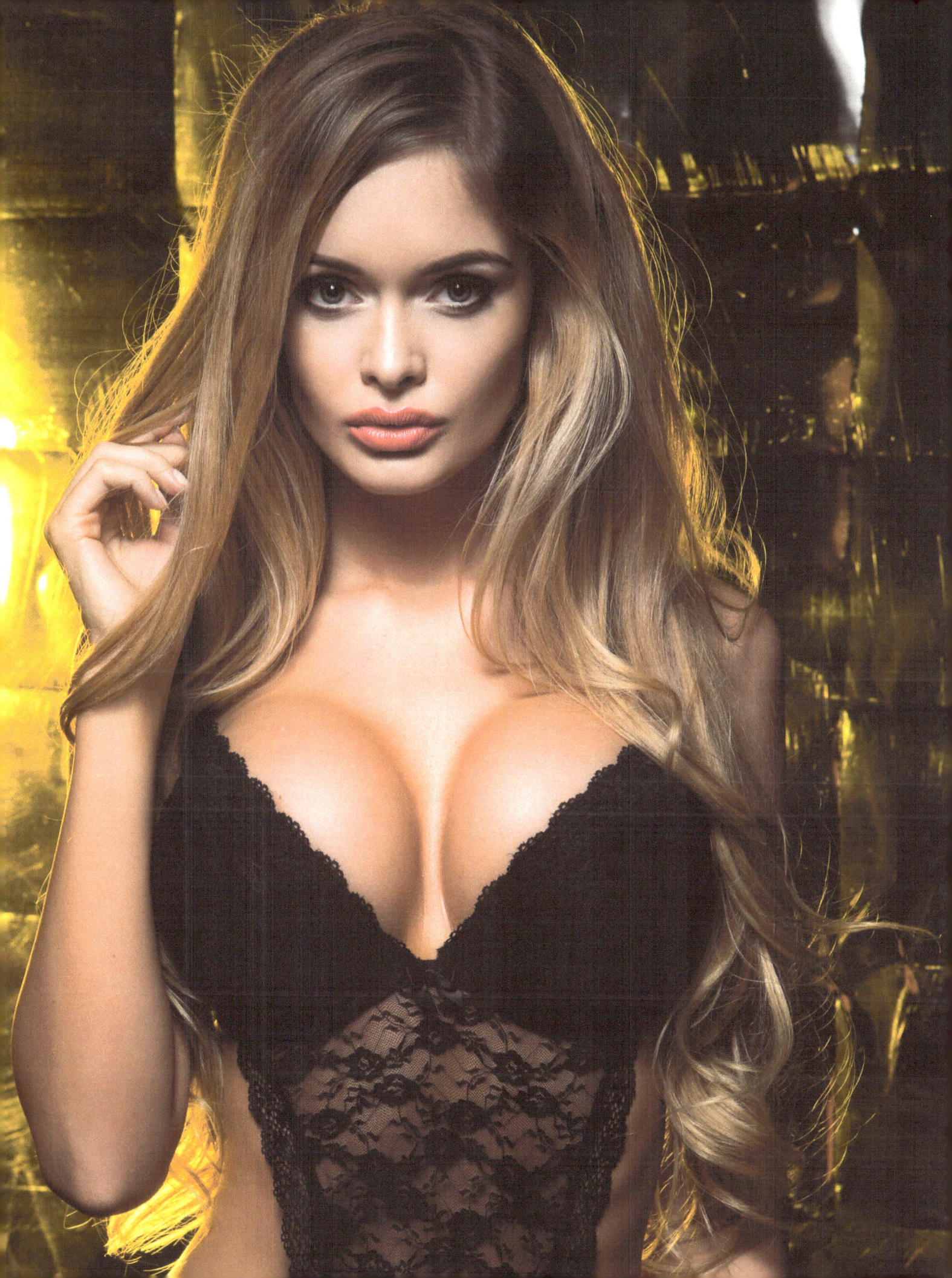

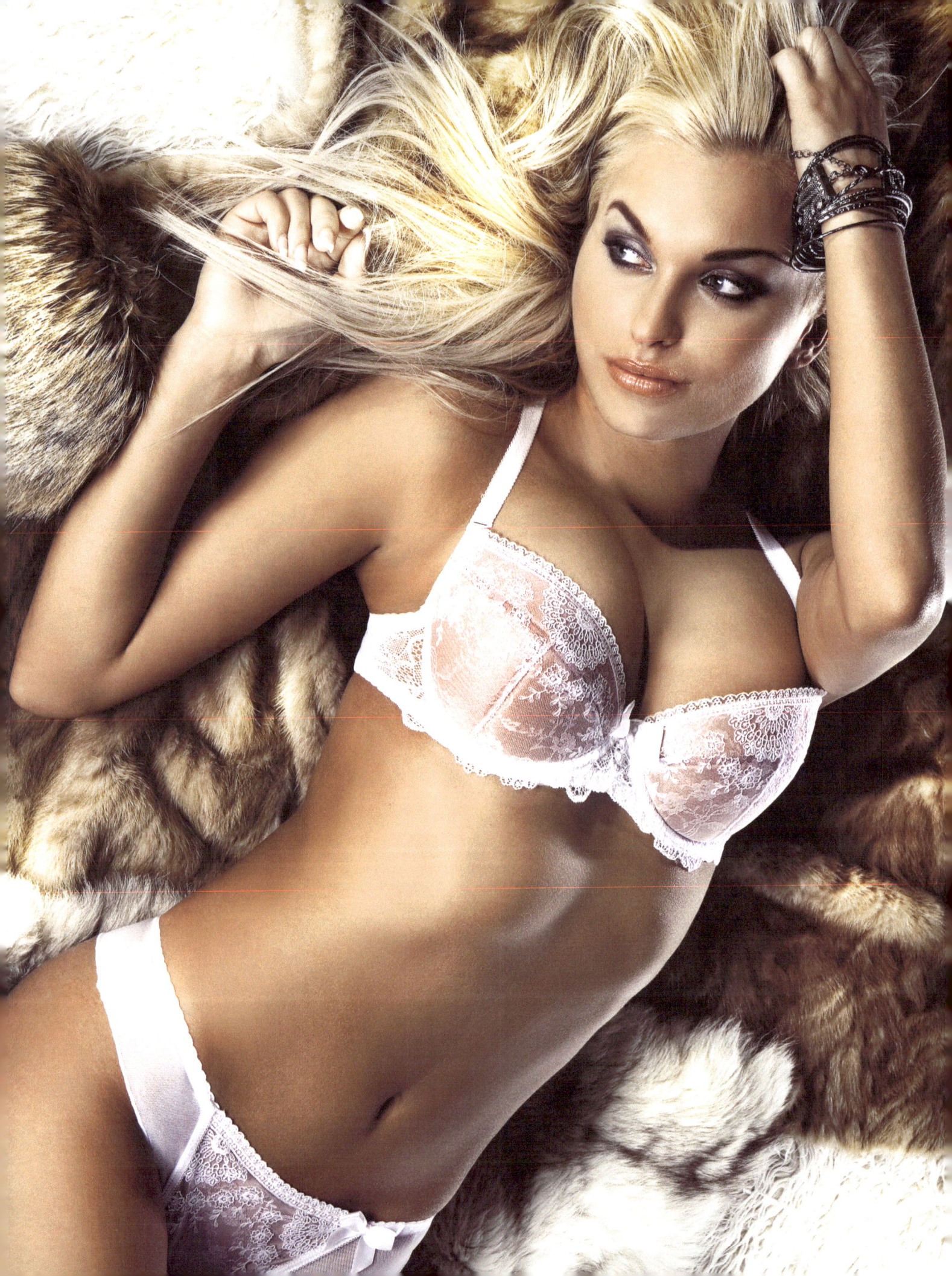

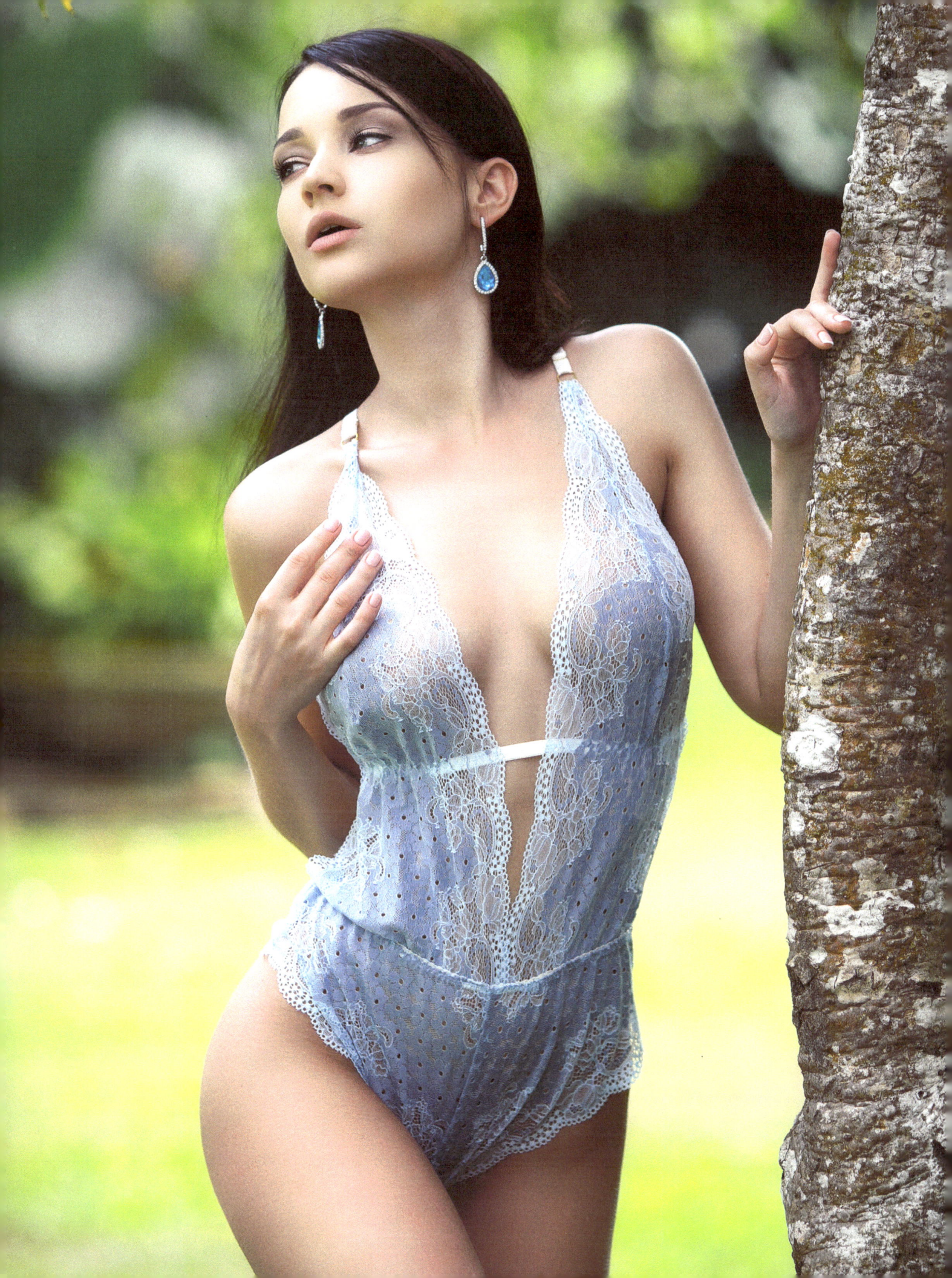

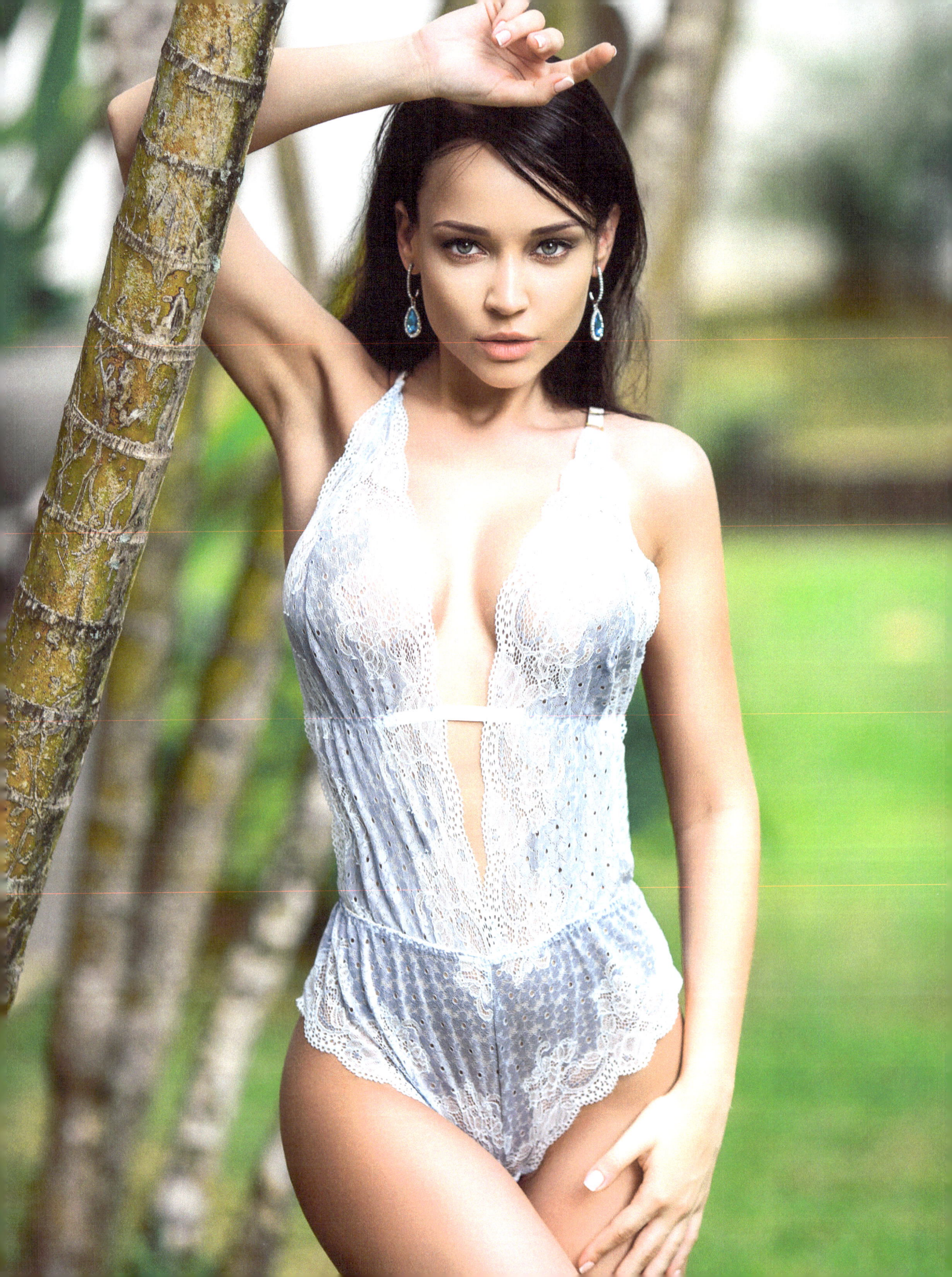

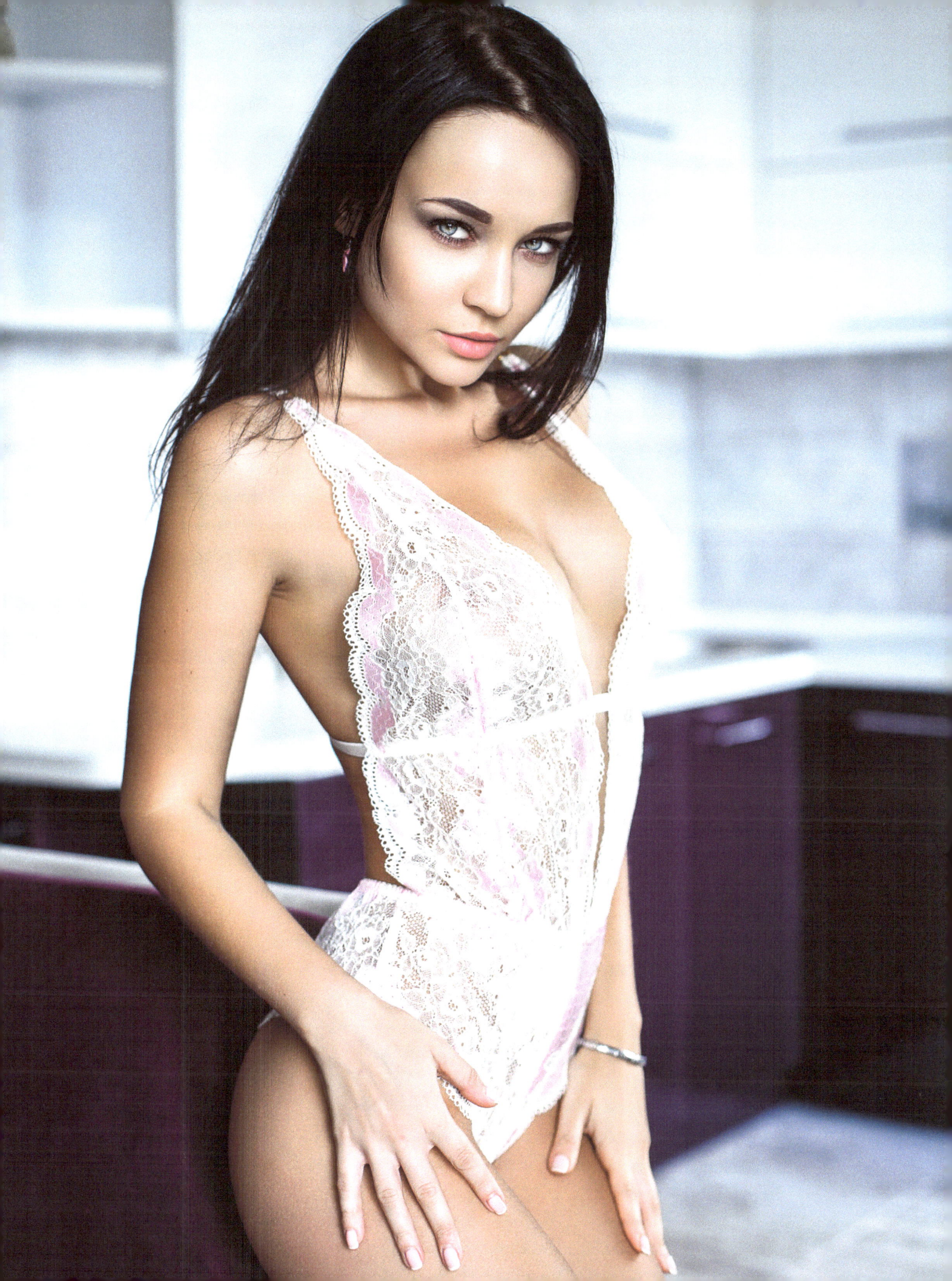

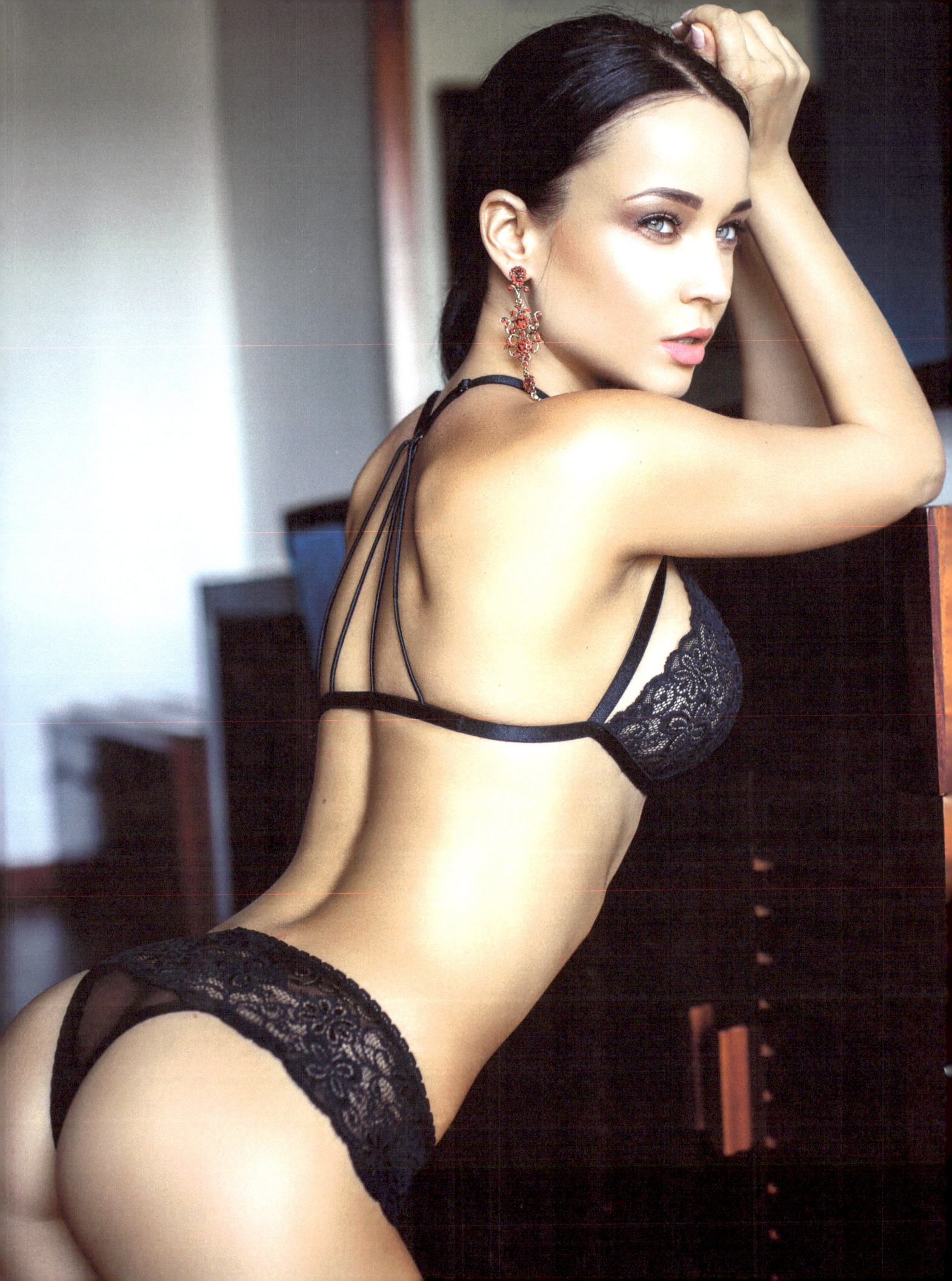

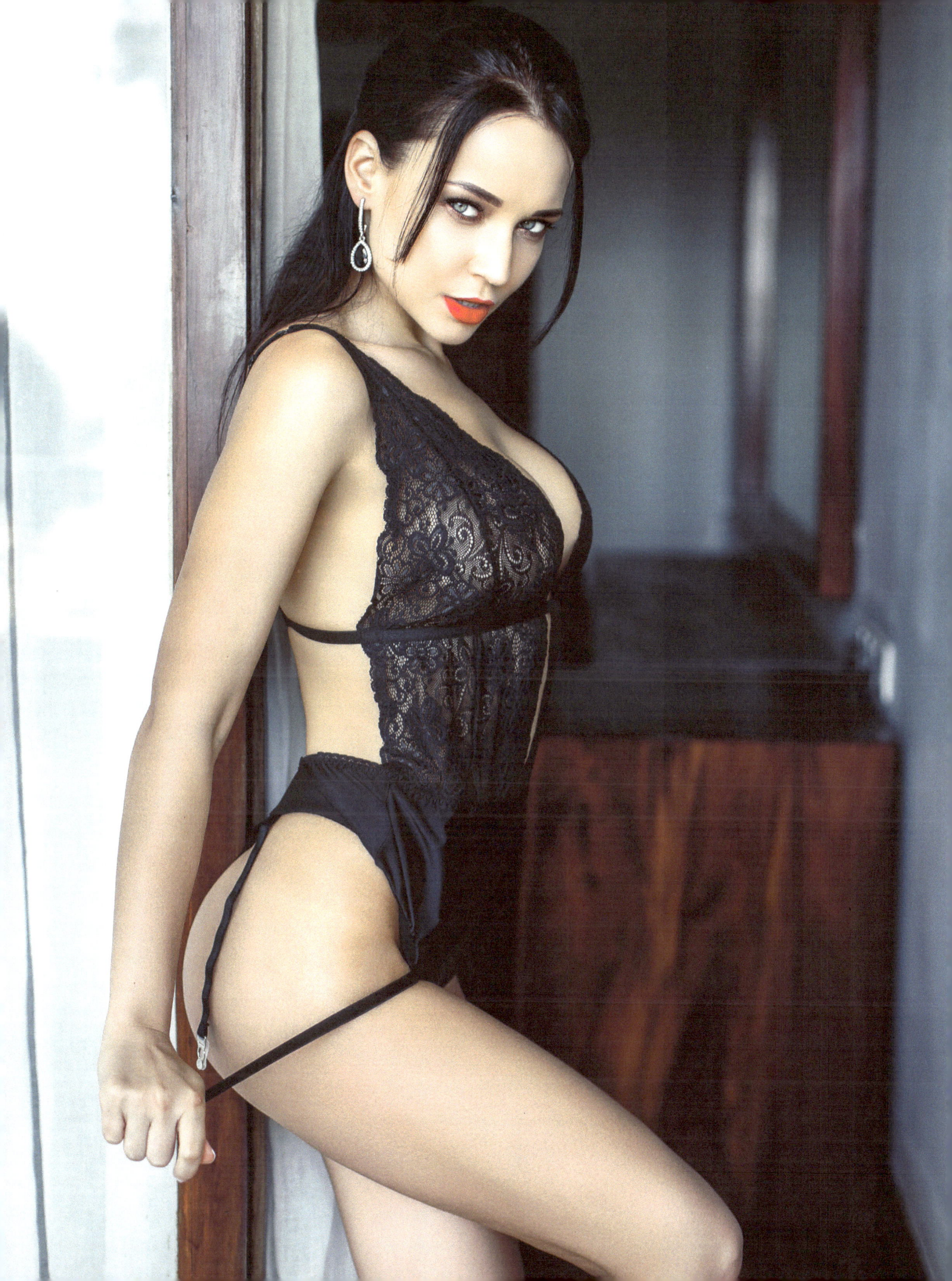

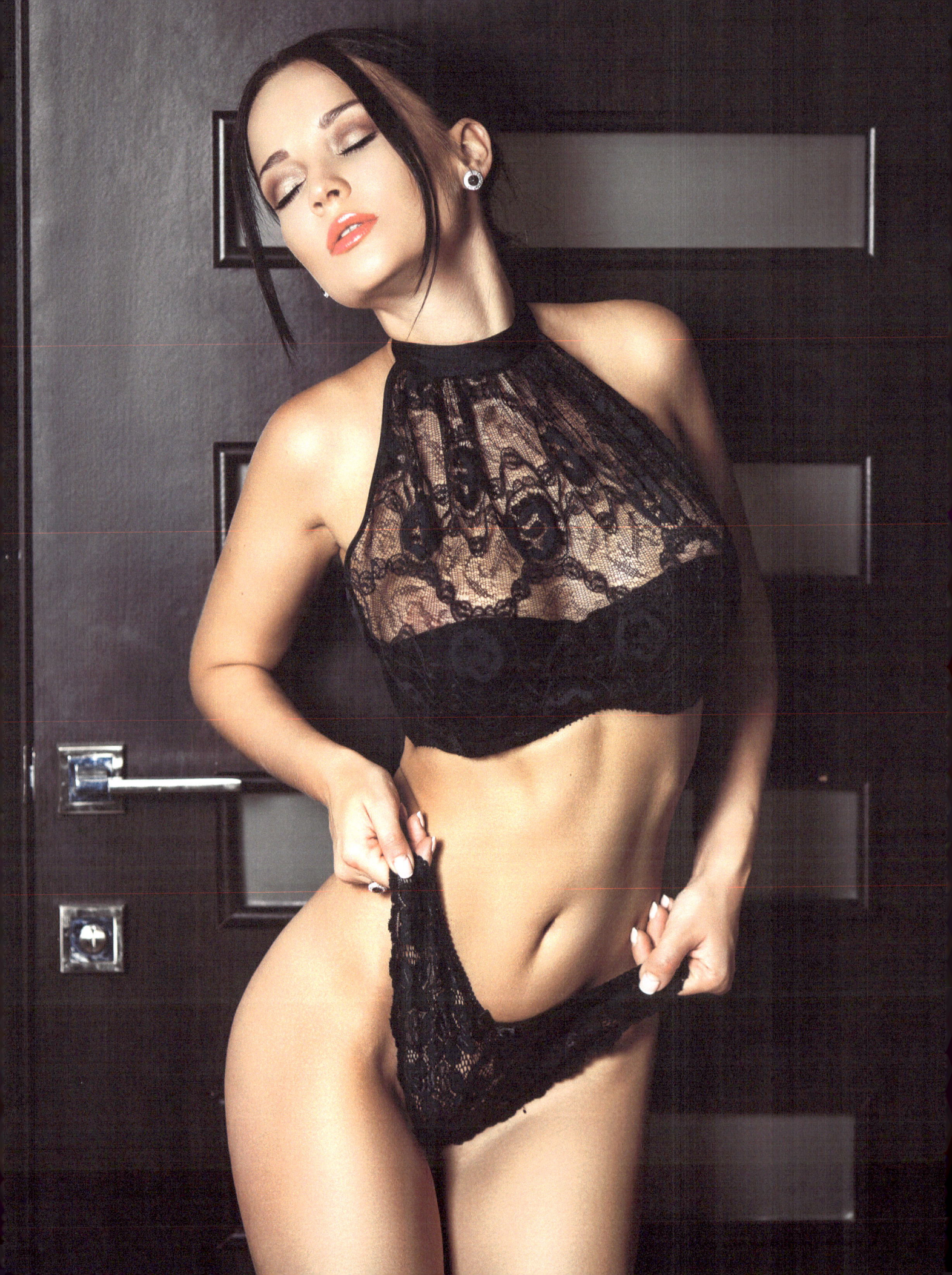

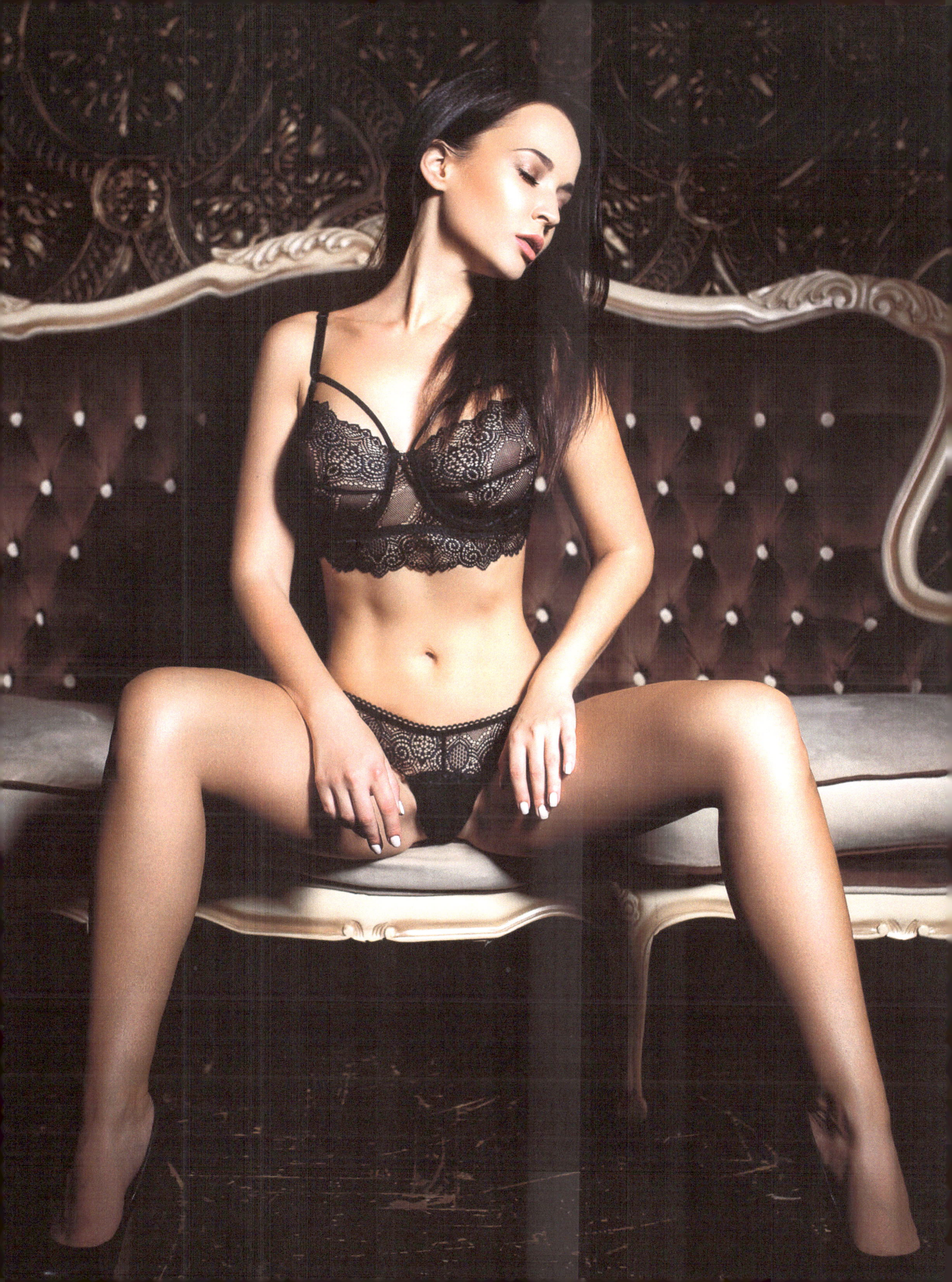

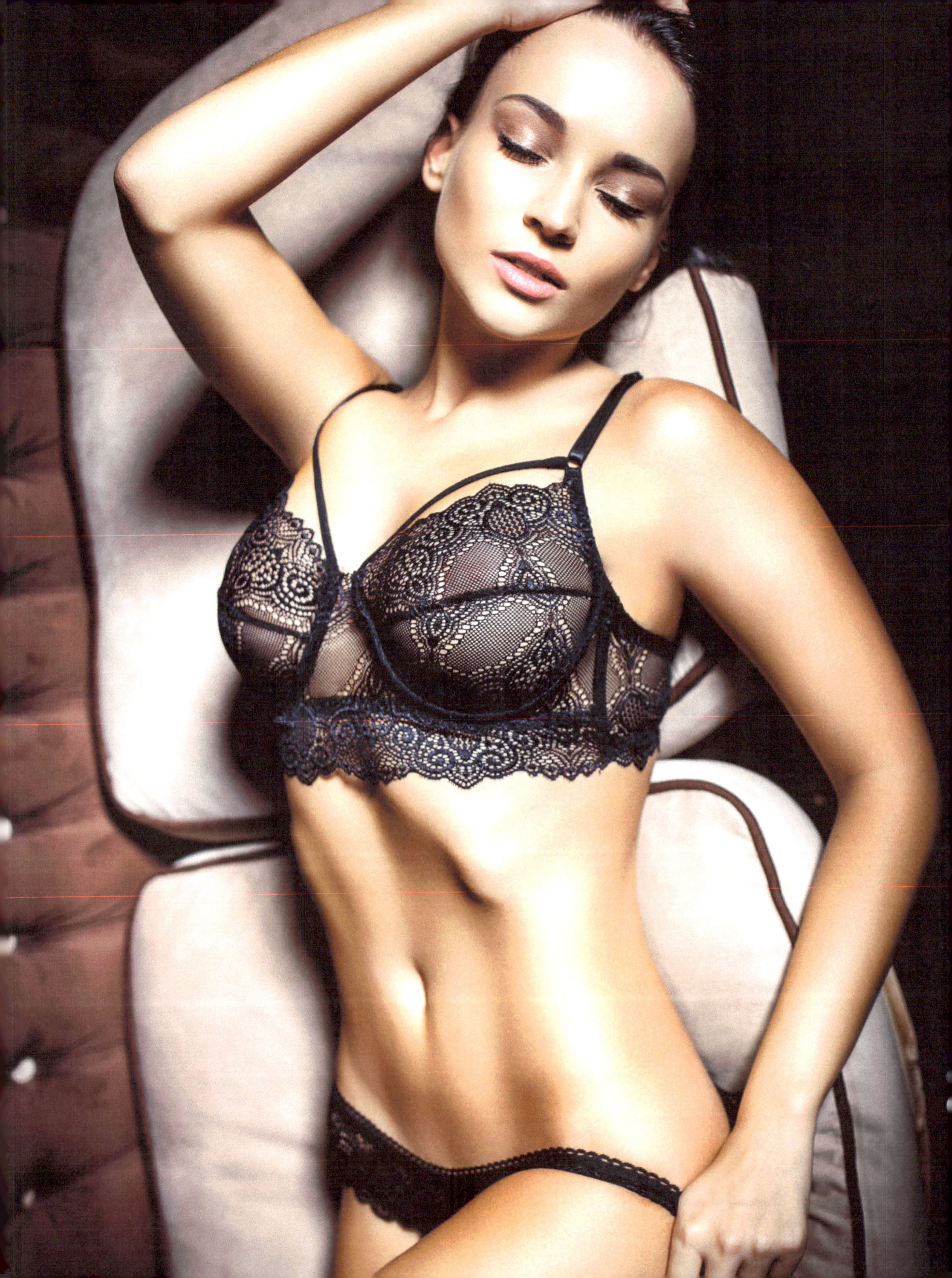

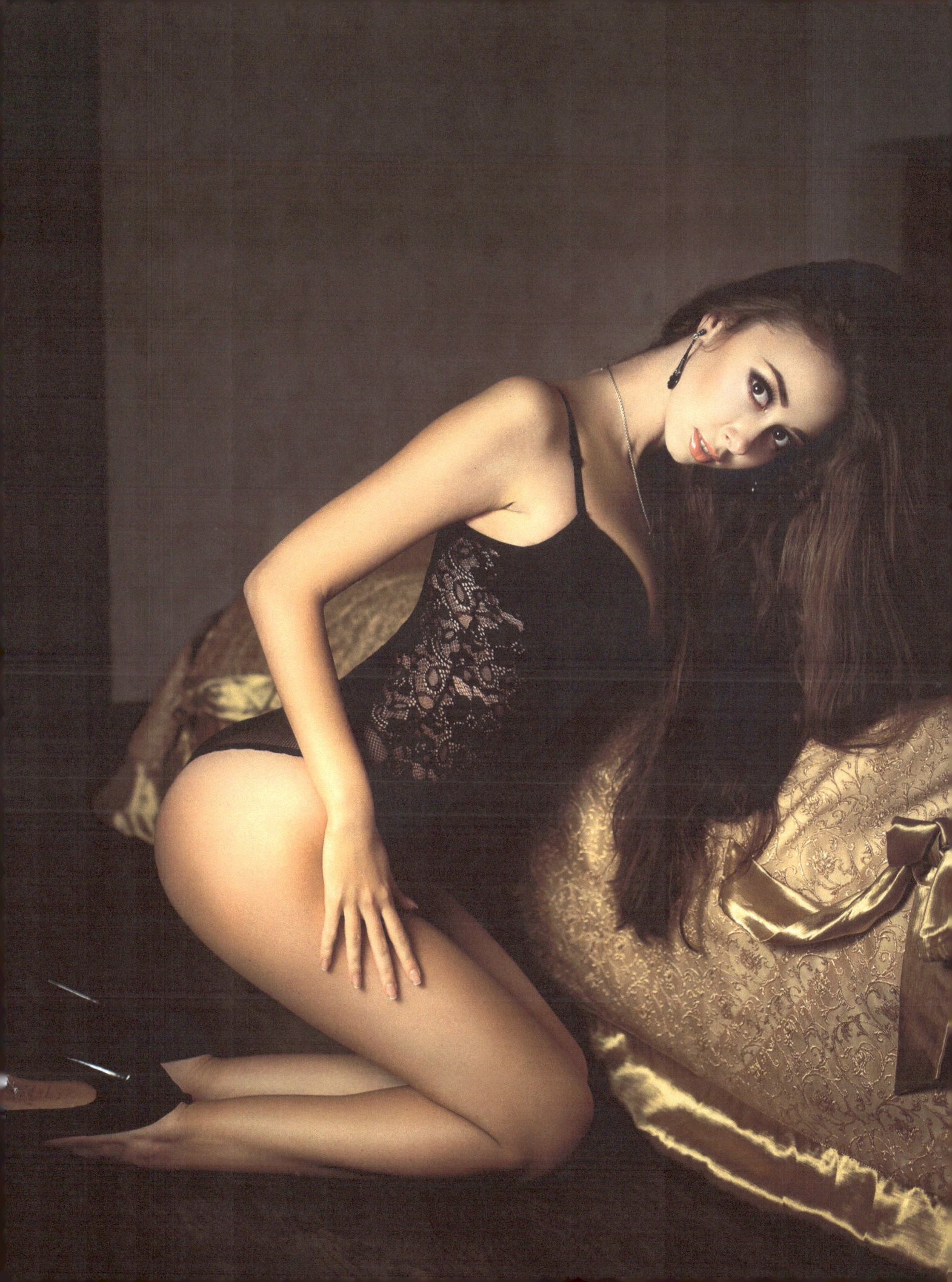

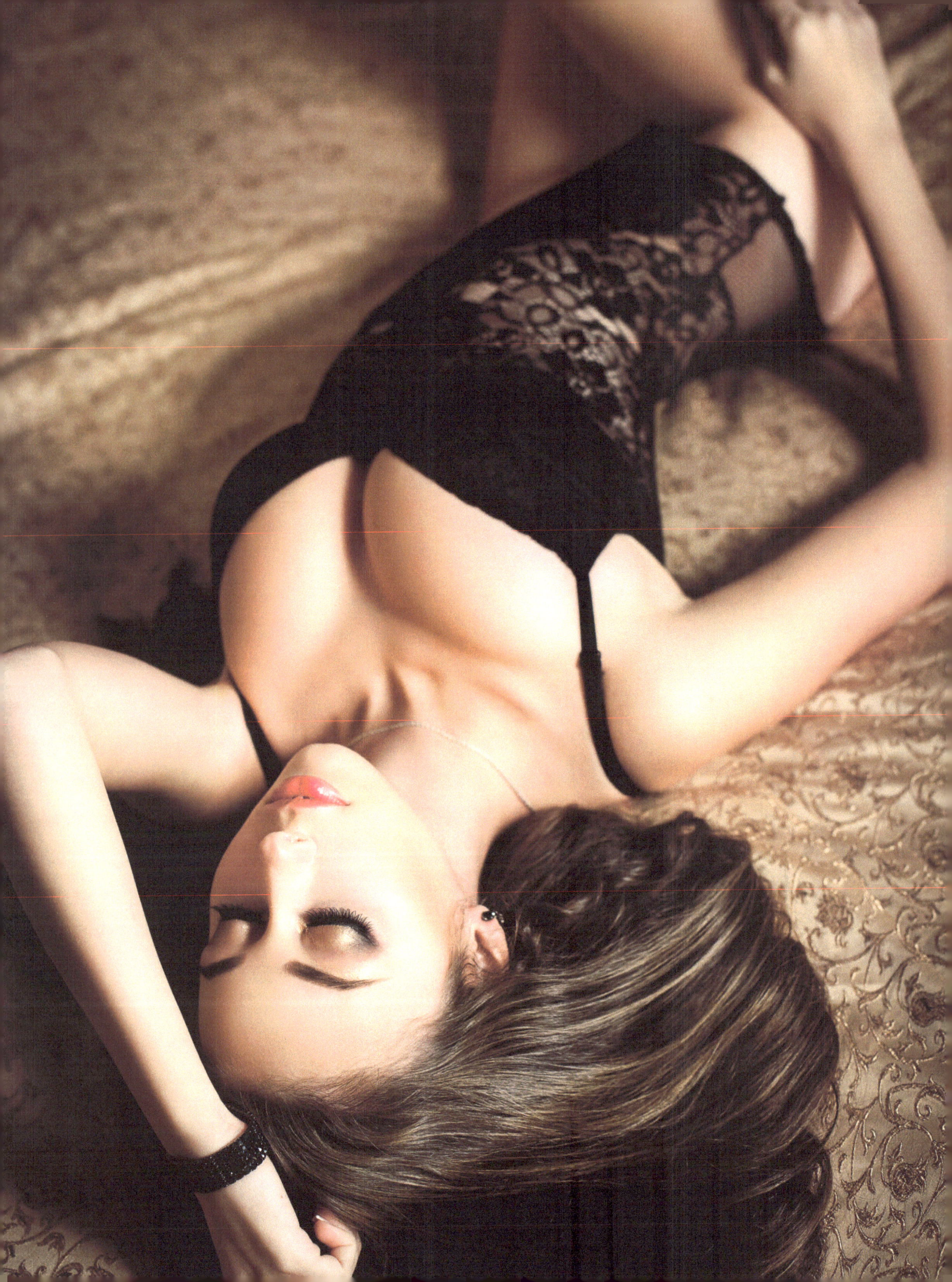

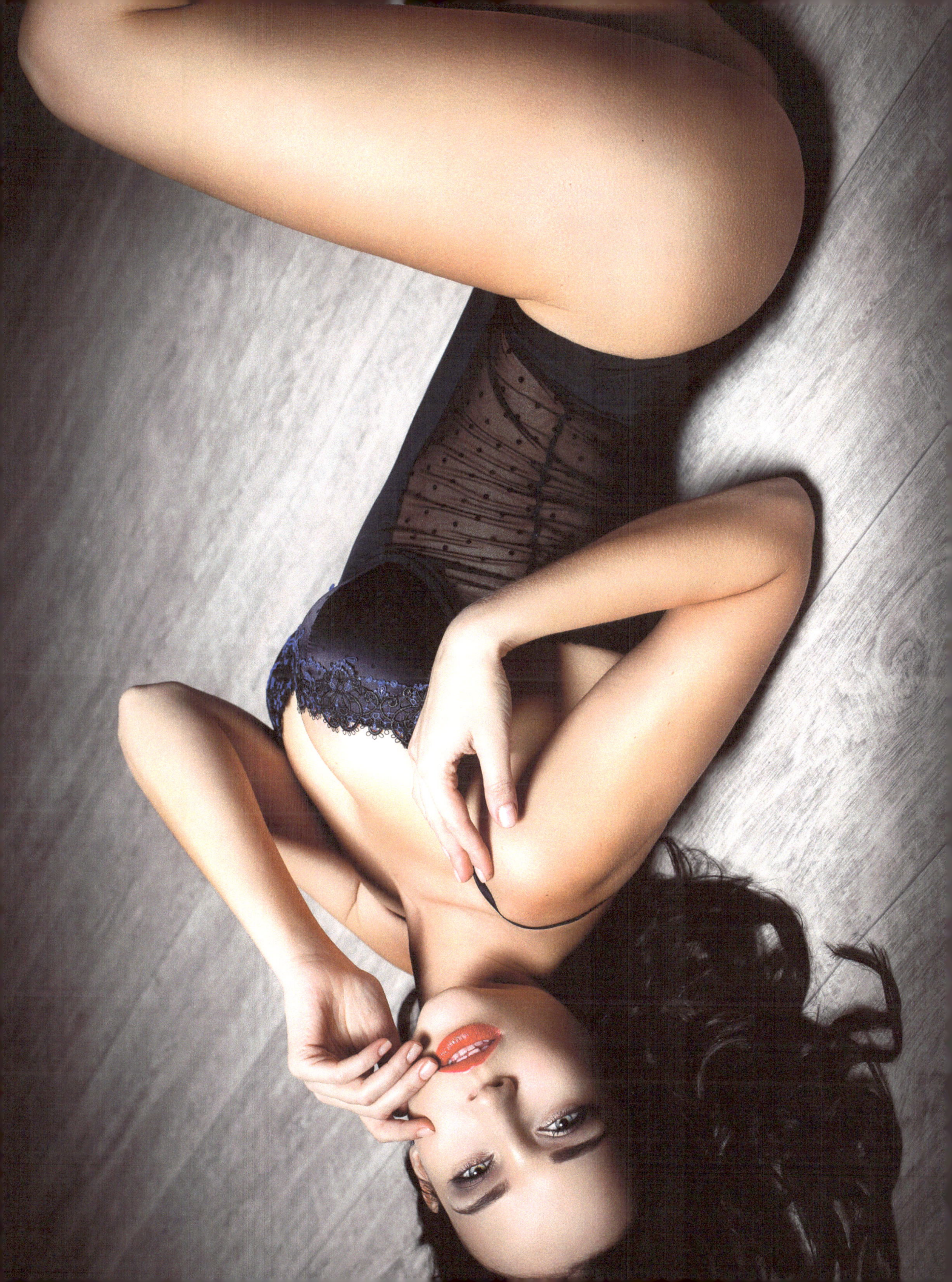

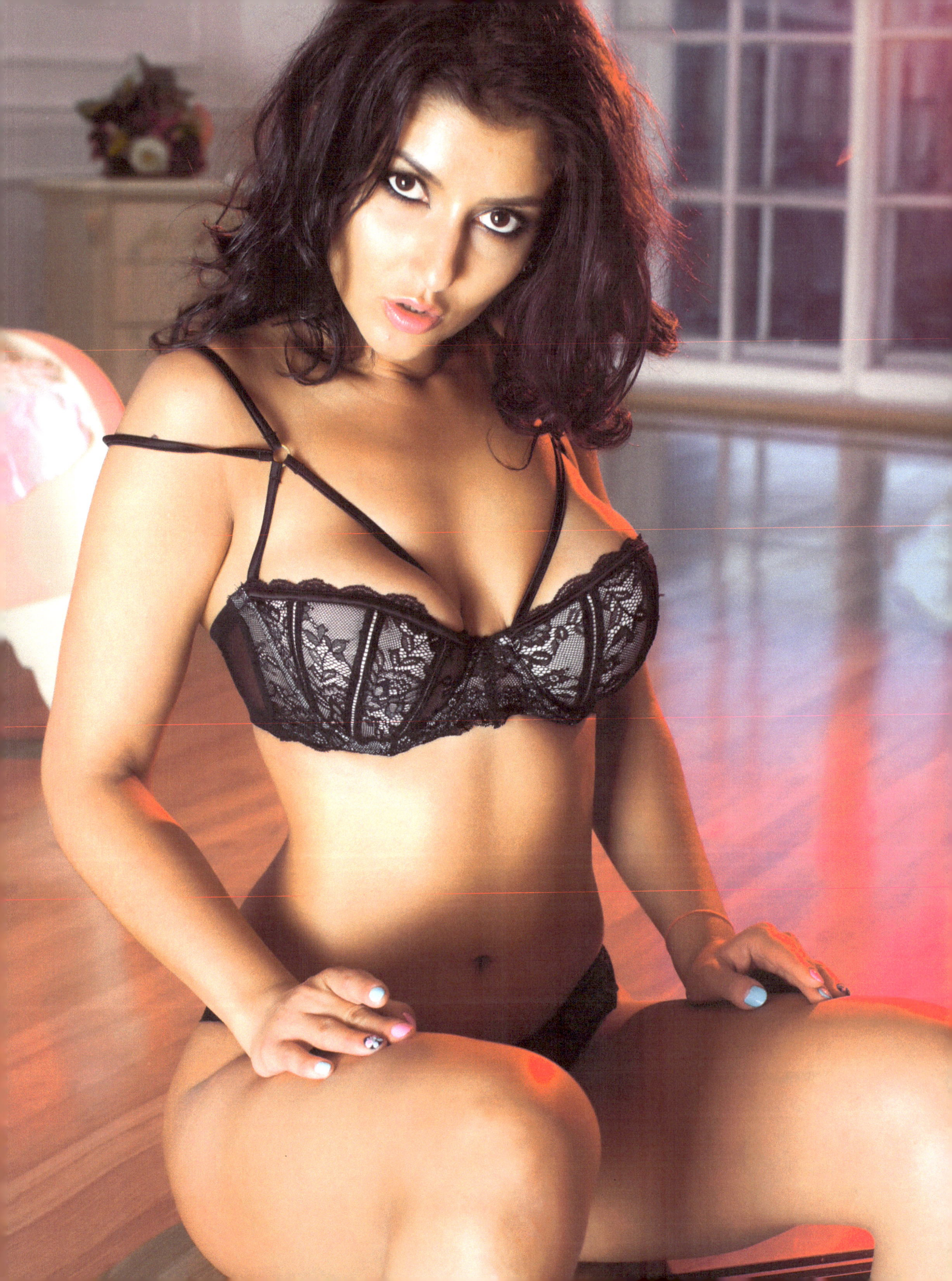

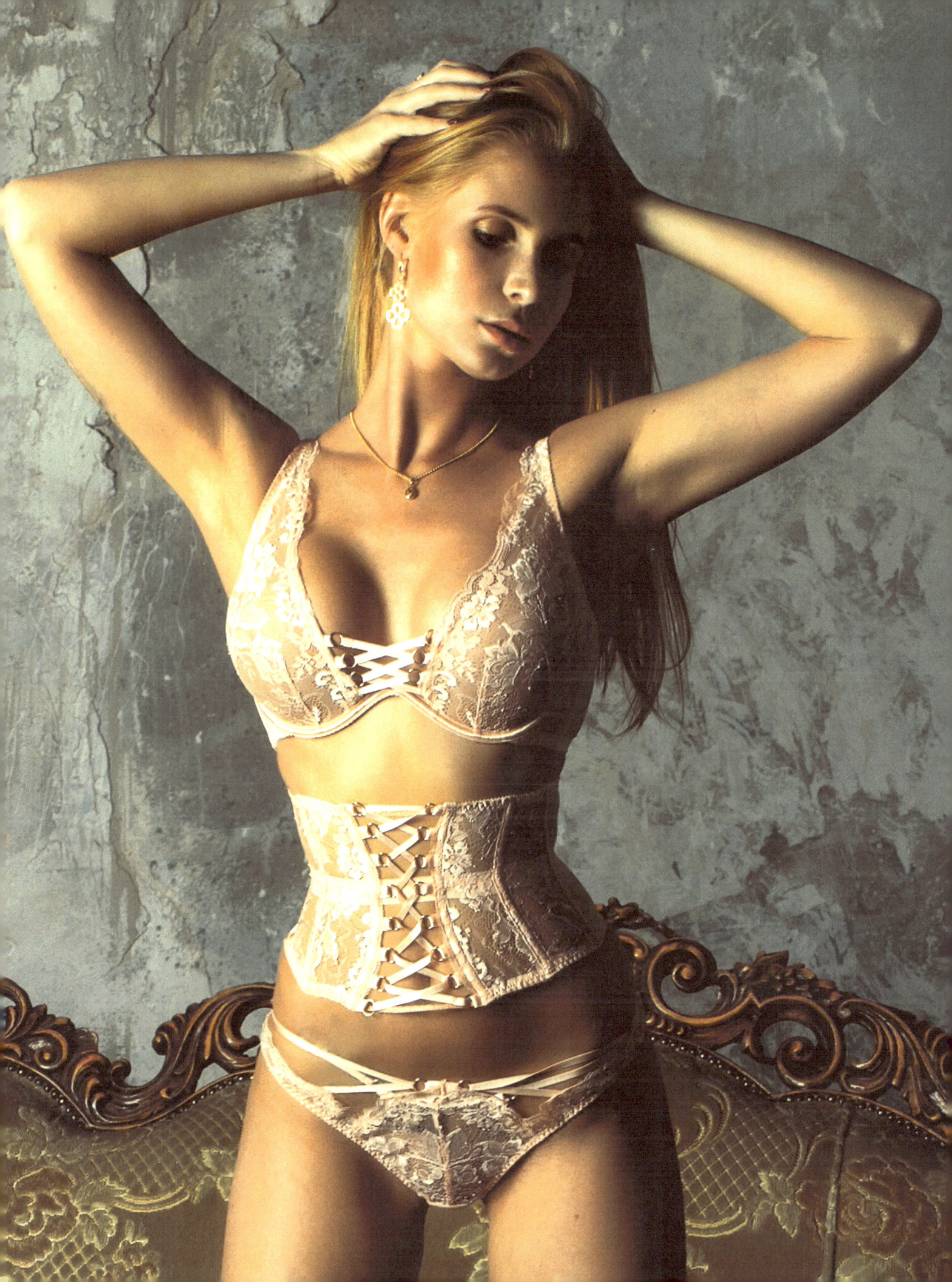

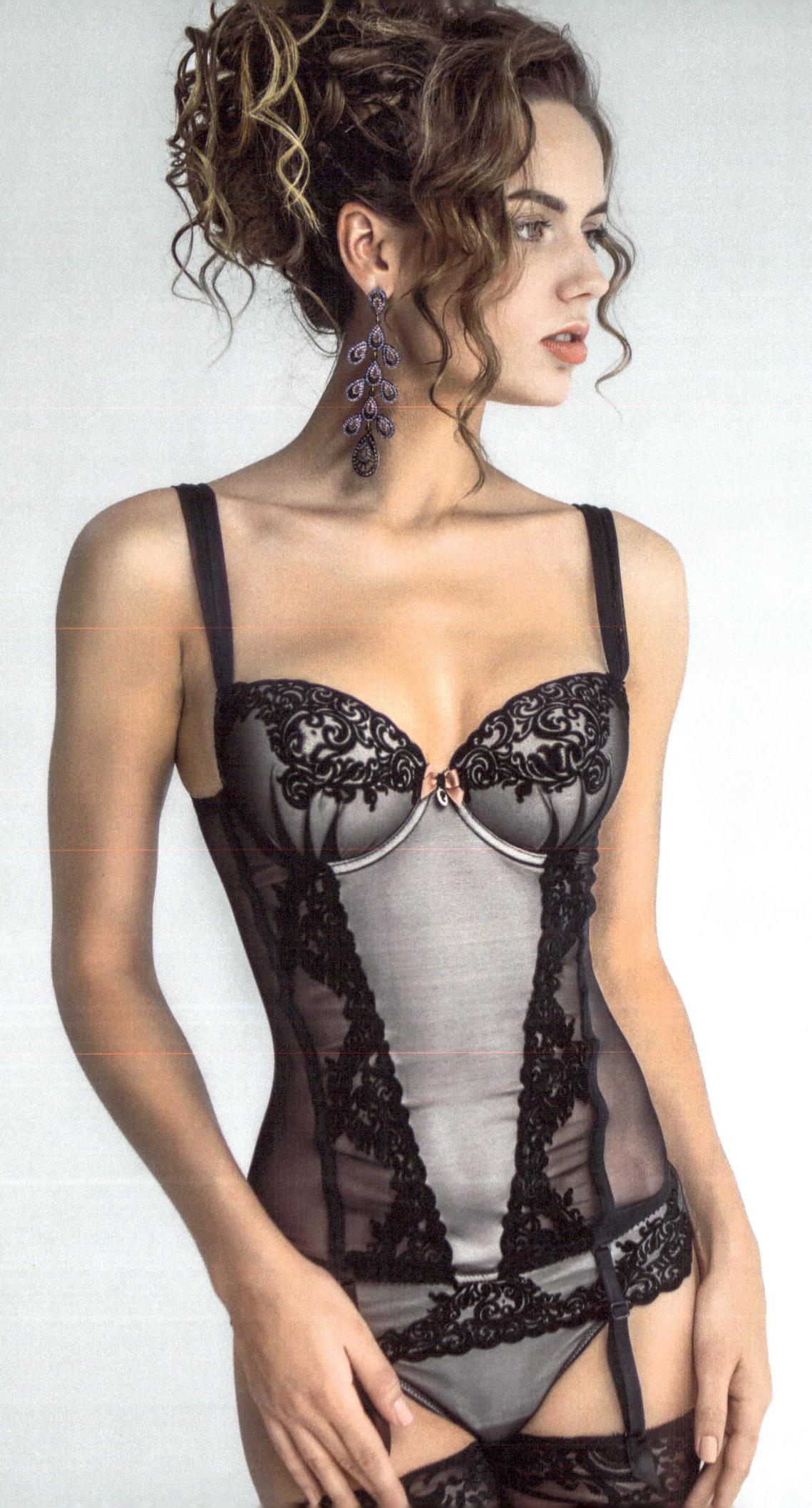

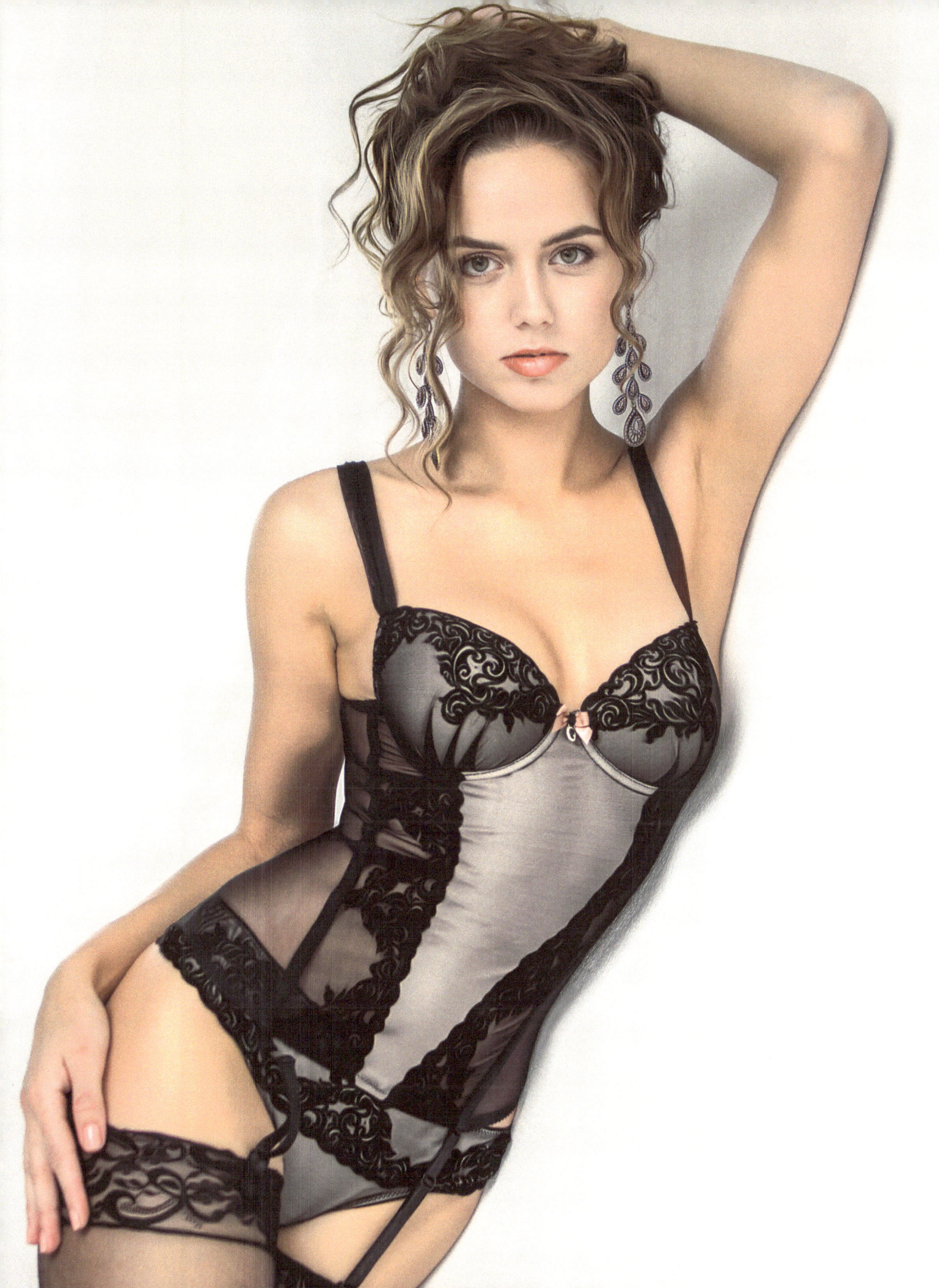

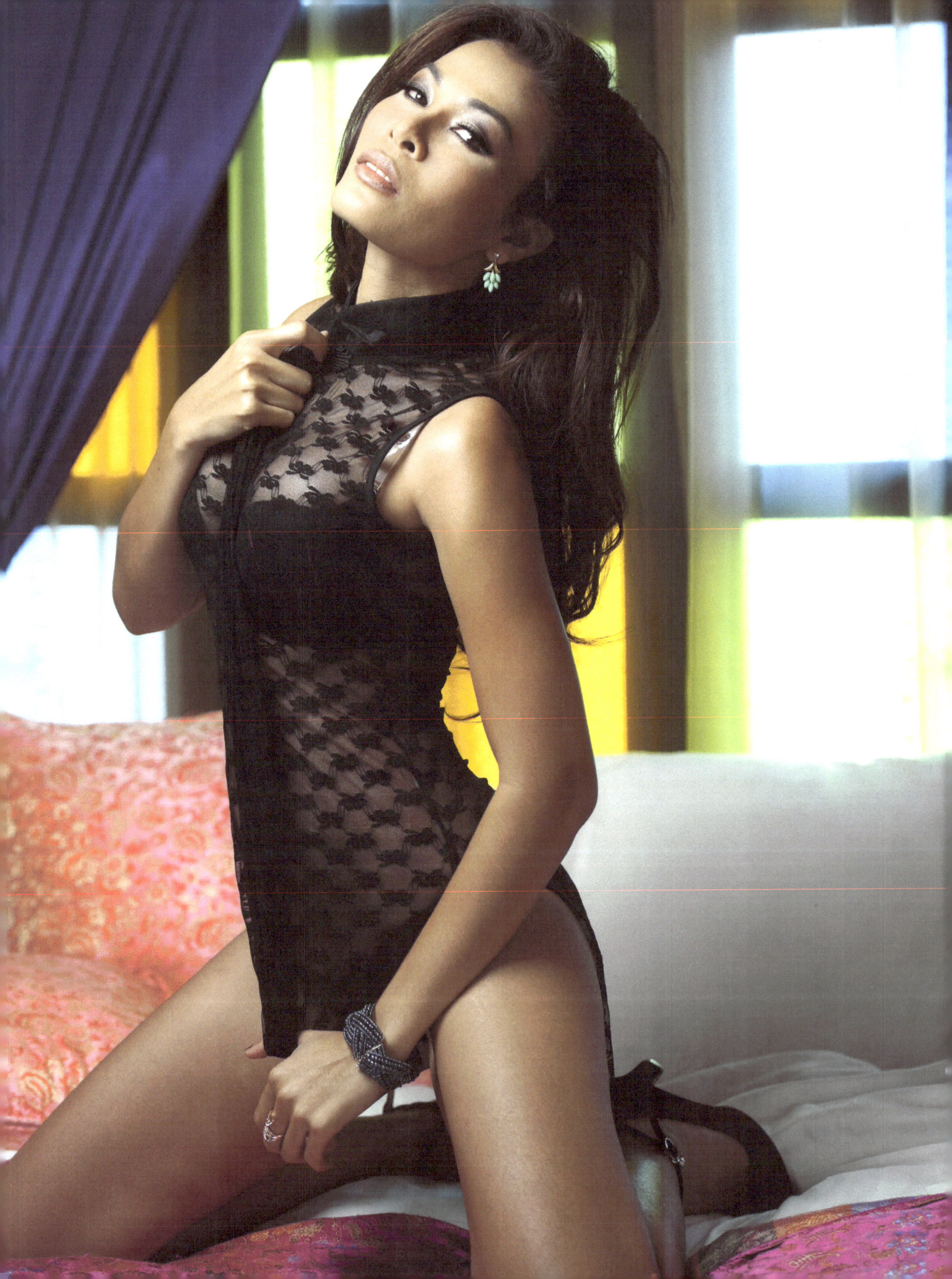

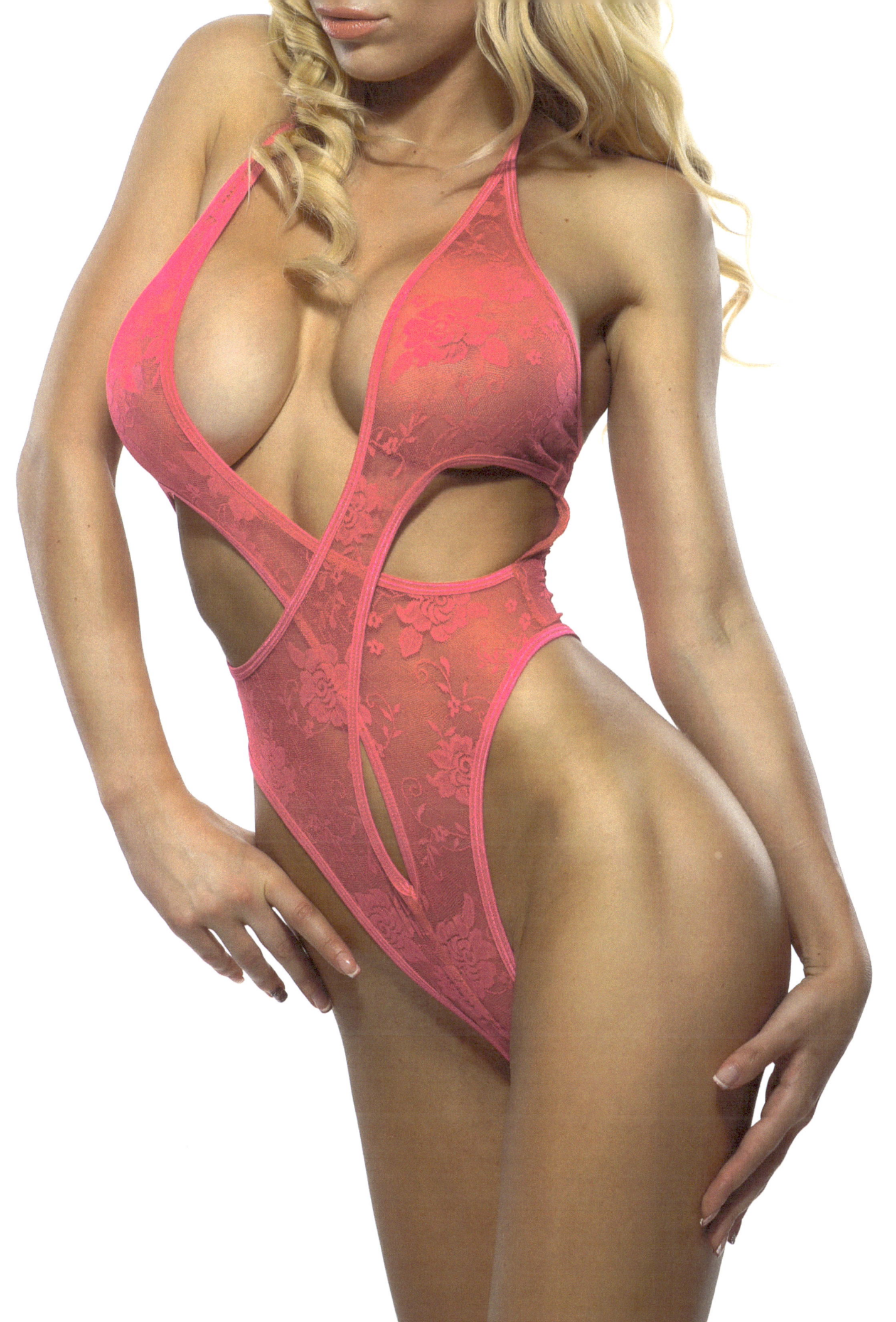

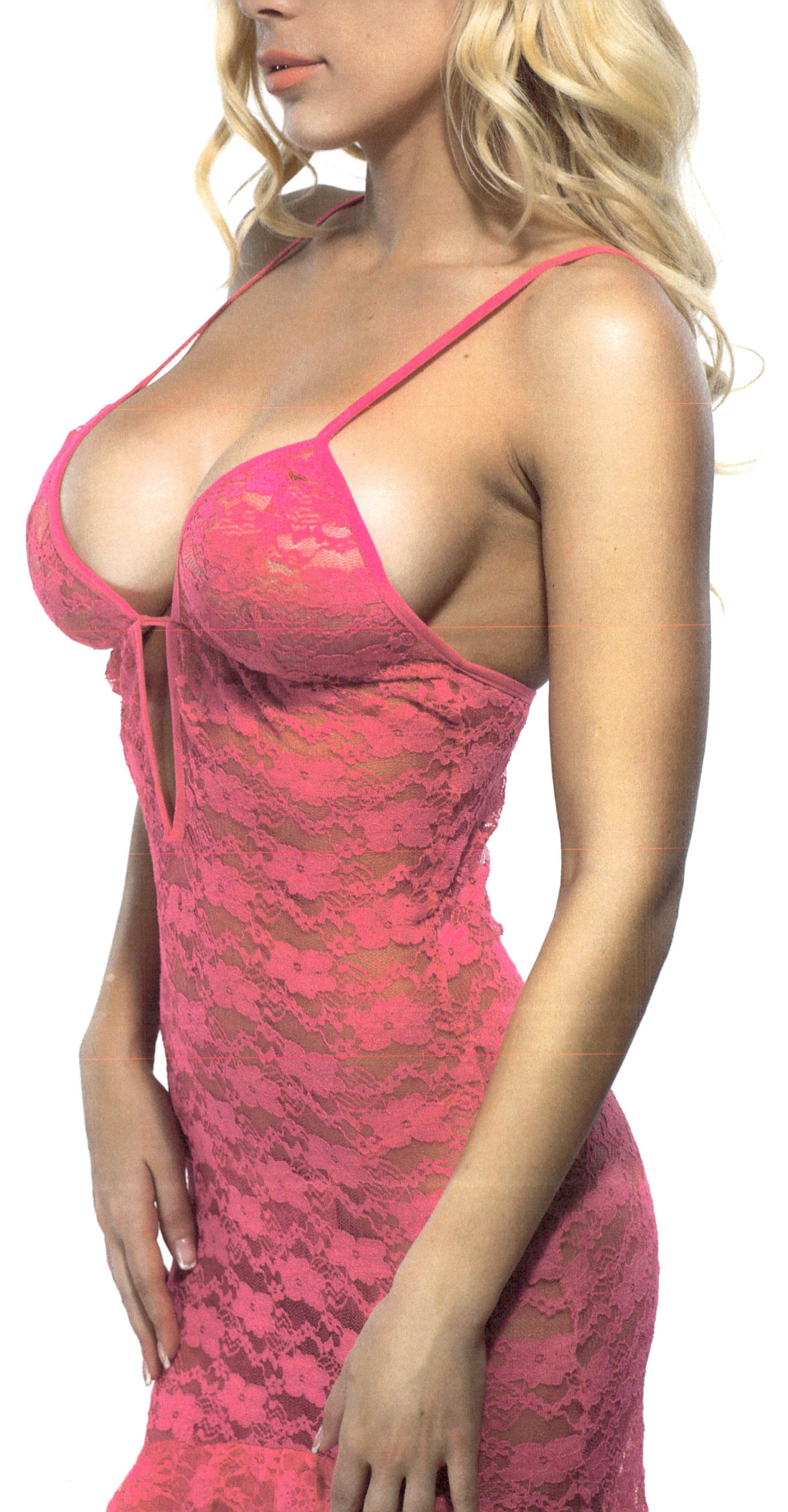

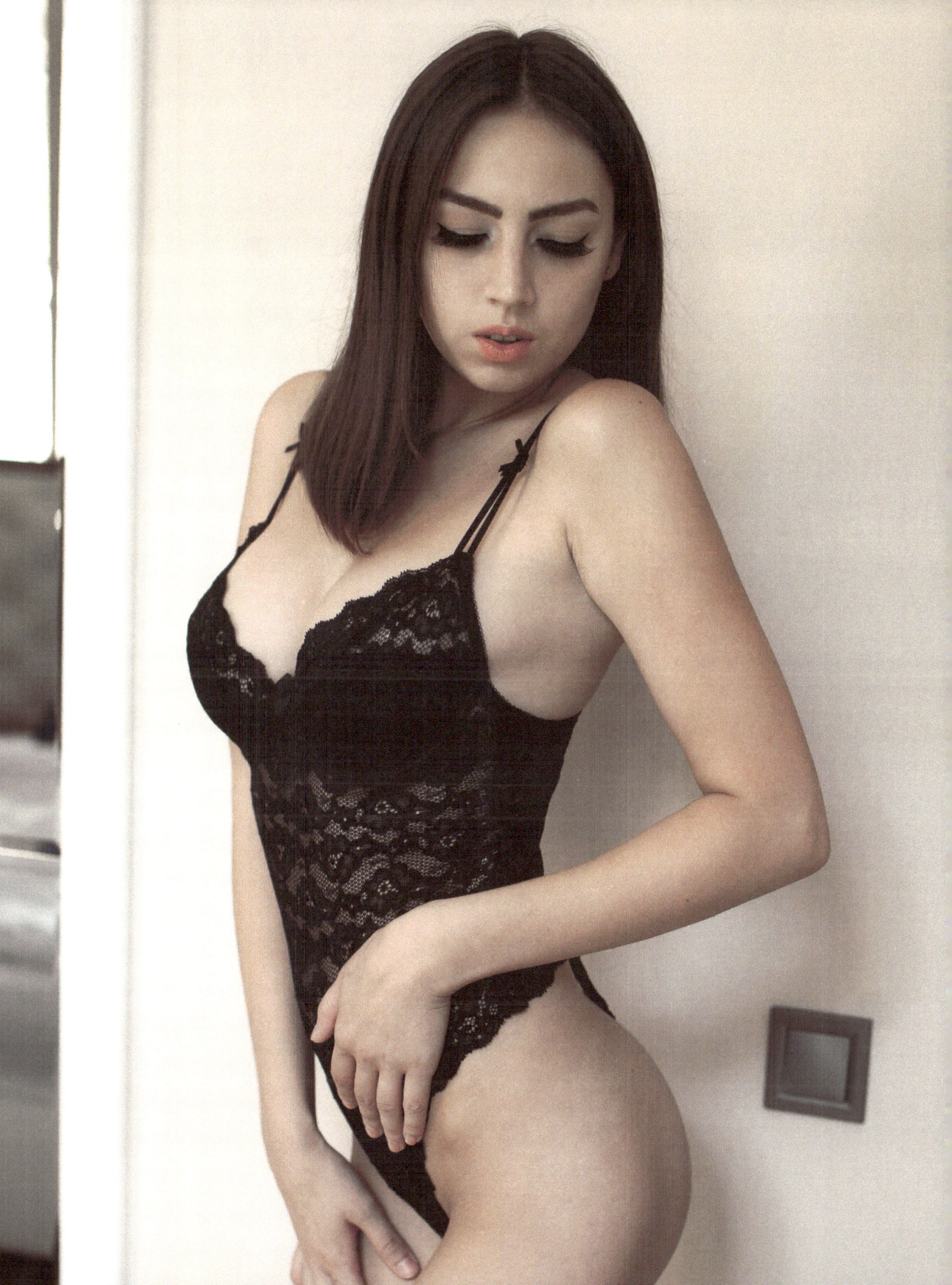

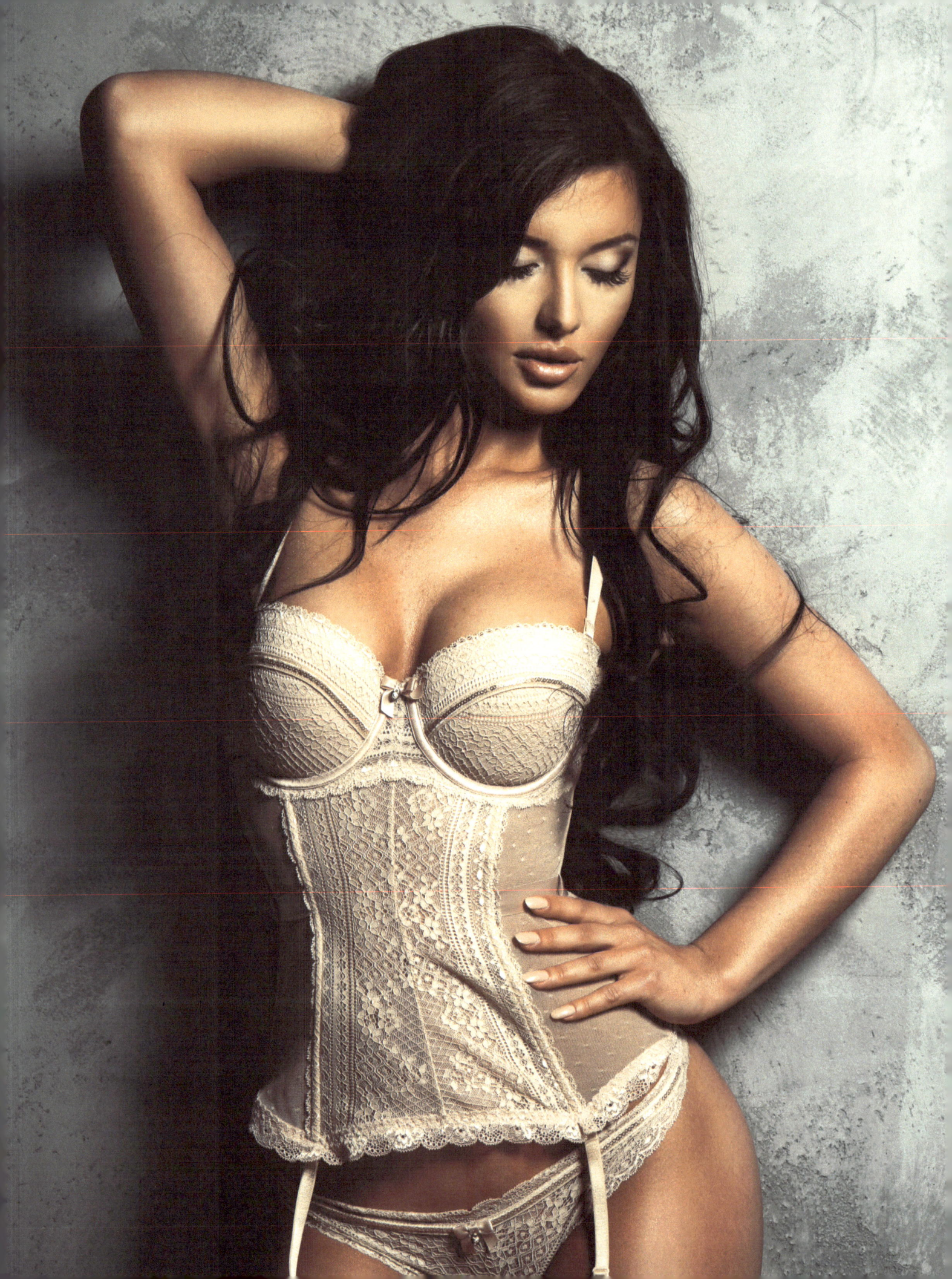

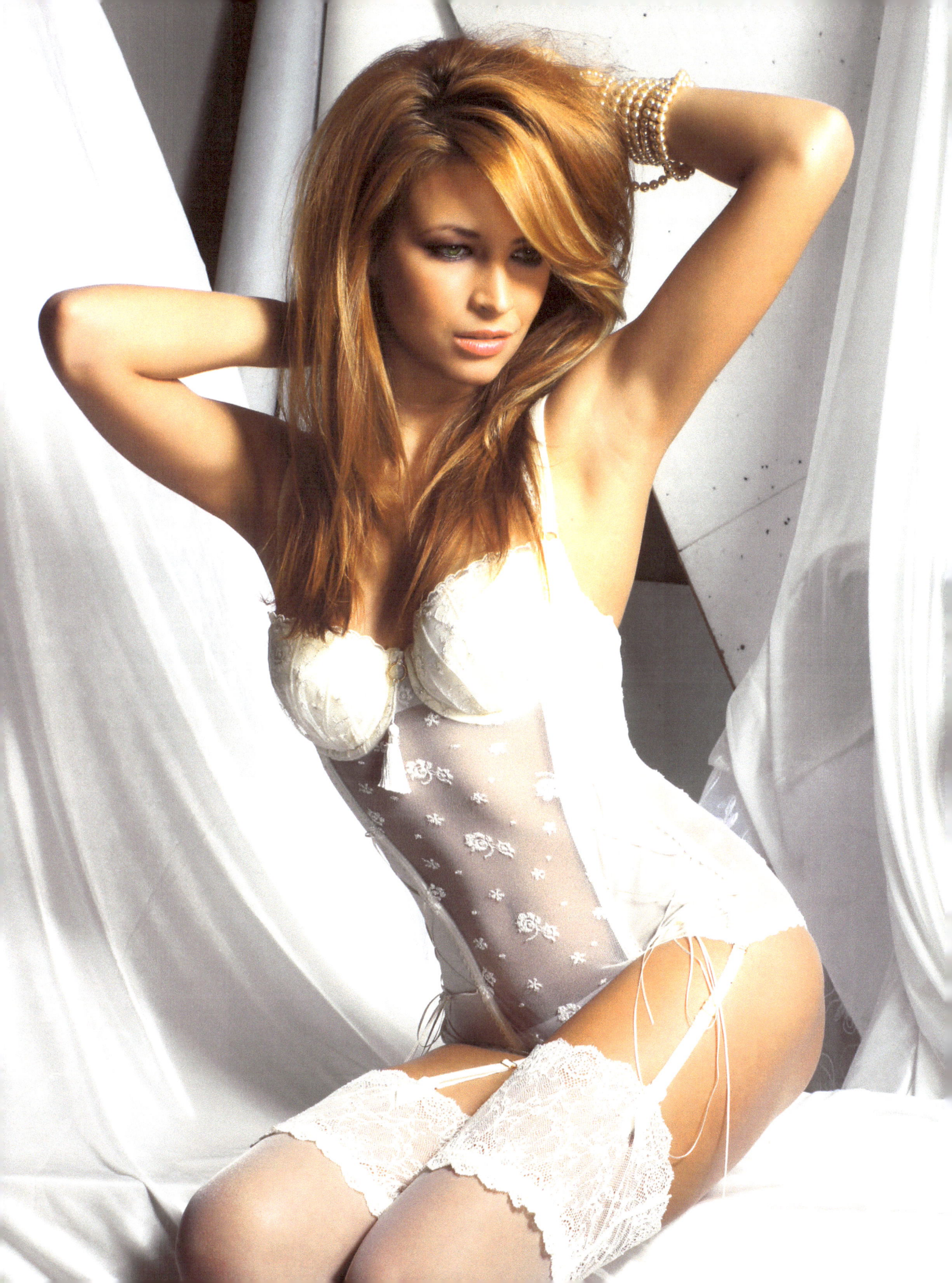

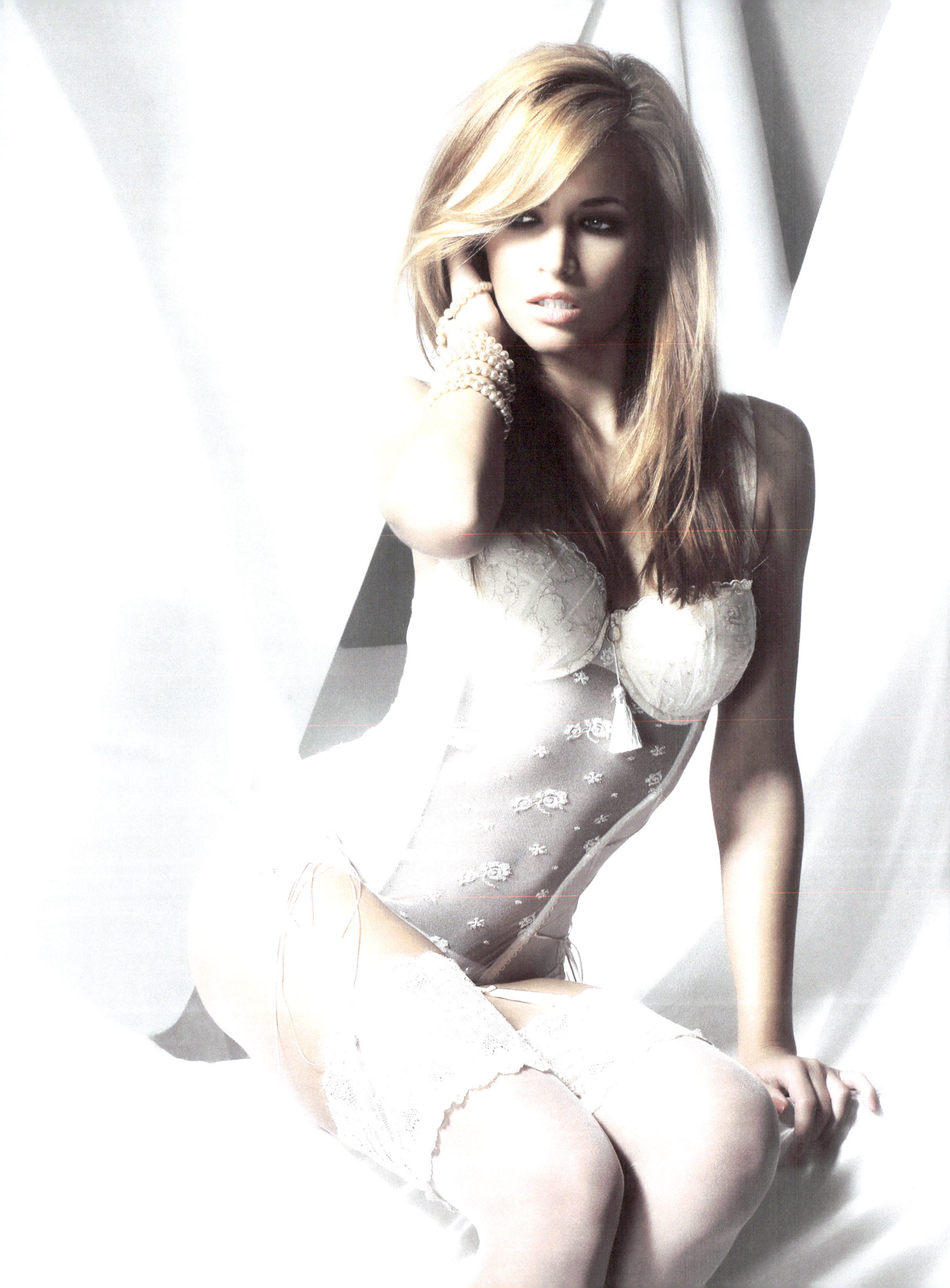

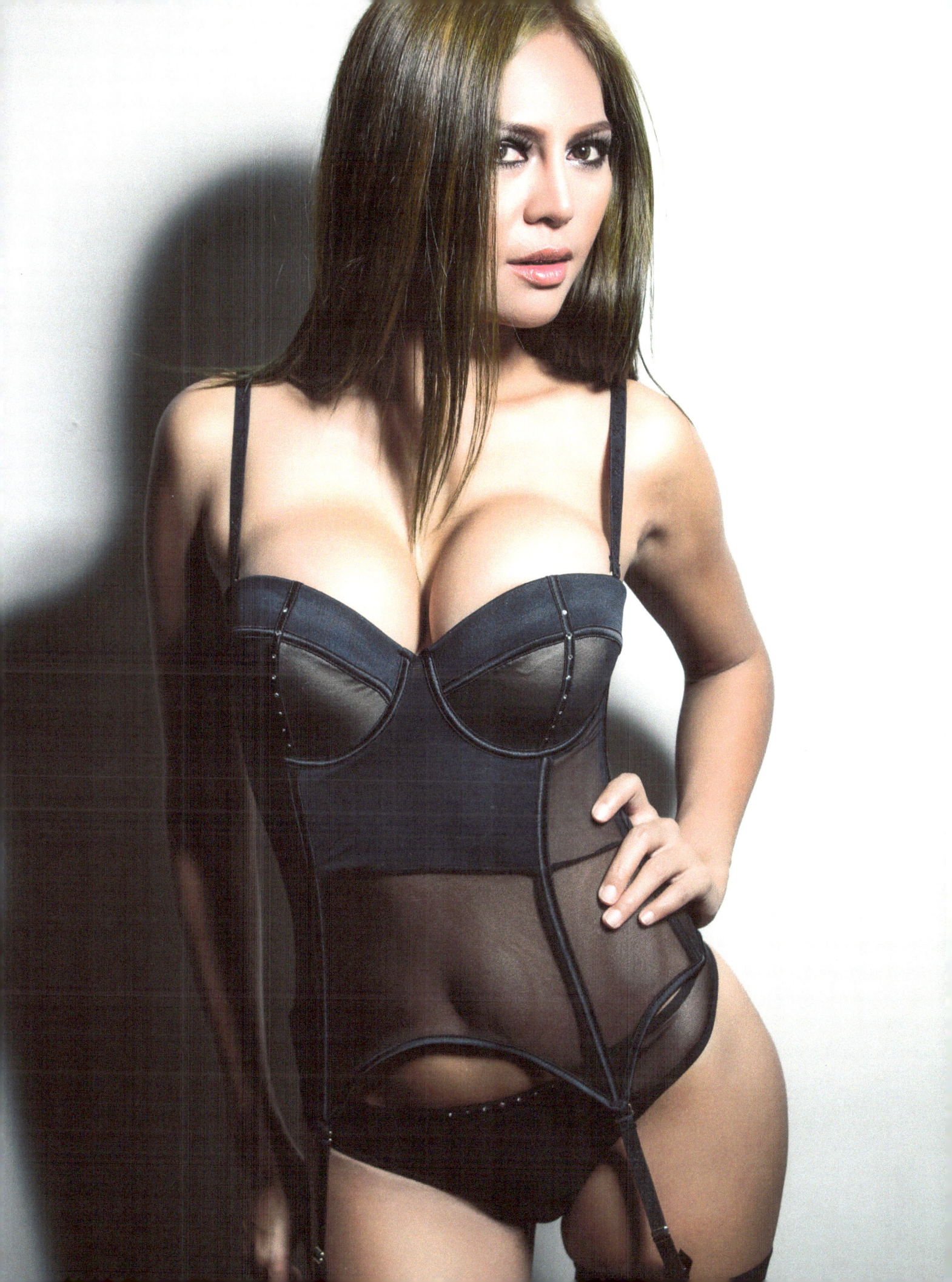

www.ingramcontent.com/pod-product-compliance
Lightning Source LLC
Chambersburg PA
CBHW050422180526
45159CB00005B/2367